Contents

The Prophet Bedward

One of the strangest tales Jamaica has to tell is the tale of the Prophet Bedward and of how the world nearly ended on the thirty-first of December 1920.

Bedward was born in the small village of August Town not far from Kingston. Instead of climbing mango trees, or playing bat and ball with the other village boys down by the river, Bedward preferred to sit at home and read the Bible. He loved to read the Bible and as he grew older he liked to gather a group of people round him and read the Bible to them. He had such a fine voice that people came from far and near to hear him. Bedward was very flattered by all this attention and soon began telling people of conversations he had with God when he was sitting in his yard at night.

Sometimes Bedward got so carried away by the sound of his own voice that he began making up stories just for the effect they had on his listeners. That was bad enough but, even worse, Bedward would then forget that he had made up the story and start believing it himself.

One night Bedward announced to his followers that the world would end on the thirty-first of December that year. Can you imagine what a fright everyone got!

'Dear brothers,' said Bedward, 'there is only one thing to be done. You must sell everything you have and give the money to me.'

One man in the village who was richer than the others because he owned a cow was unhappy at this thought.

'If the world is going to end on the thirty-first of December then why should we give the money to you? What good can it do you?' he asked.

'Ah, dear friend,' replied Bedward, 'on the thirty-first of December I shall fly up to Heaven and all my followers with me. Whoever gives me his money or his goods can claim them again in Heaven.'

The rich man rather liked this idea and so did many of the villagers. They went home and sold their land and their houses, and their pigs and their goats, and their mules and their donkeys. They sold their tables and their chairs, and pots and pans, and brooms and coconut brushes, and gourds and yabas.

Now Bedward told his followers not to let anyone else know that the world was about to end since he could not take everyone to Heaven with him, but somehow the news leaked out.

It was an old woman with only four eggs to sell who let the secret out. The four eggs were all she had in the world.

'When him and me fly up to Heaven,' she told the man who was buying the eggs, 'I want to be sure to have my h'eggs to make an h'omelette.'

By the first of December, huge crowds began to

gather at August Town. They prayed by day and they prayed by night. Bedward read the Bible to them and warned that the end of the world was near. The newspapers carried the story from end to end of Jamaica and all over the country people began selling their houses and their land, their pigs and their goats, their mules and their donkeys, their pots and pans, brooms and coconut brushes, their gourds and their yabas. The newspapers warned that the country's economy would be ruined if this panic selling went on.

Meanwhile Bedward was sitting by the river in August Town with his followers. He baptised them in the river to wash away their sins. Bakers baked bread and gave it away free. Old women boiled yams to share with the crowd. Everyone had sold all they had. The government sent police and soldiers to the area to guard against any trouble, but many of the police and soldiers were so impressed by Bedward that they sold their belts and their boots, and their helmets and their rifles, and sat down on the ground with Bedward's followers to await the end of the world.

On the night of the thirty-first of December no one slept at all. Everyone stayed awake singing and chanting. Bedward told them that the world would end at six o'clock on New Year's morning. He climbed into the branches of a big mango tree that grew beside the river and announced that when six o'clock came he would jump from the topmost branch of this mango tree and be carried up to Heaven.

During the night the soldiers and the policemen

who had remained at their posts gathered round the foot of the mango tree with a big blanket. If Bedward didn't make it to Heaven they knew where he would go instead.

Just before six o'clock the next morning Bedward climbed higher and higher in the tree until he reached the topmost branch. He raised his hand to bless the kneeling crowds. As the first rays of the sun came up from behind the hill Bedward stretched out both his arms and jumped. . . .

He jumped high in the air and people gasped. For a moment it looked as though he were indeed going upward to Heaven. Then, alas, Bedward began to come down very rapidly. People screamed and ran from the foot of the tree, all except the soldiers and policemen. They held firmly to the sides of the blanket until with a mighty swoosh Bedward had fallen right in the middle of the blanket.

Poor Bedward. They took him first to prison and then to an asylum for the insane where he spent the rest of his days.

As you can imagine there was great anger and disappointment among his followers and everyone blamed everyone else for advising them to sell their houses and their lands, their pigs and their goats, their mules and their donkeys, their tables and chairs, pots and pans, brooms and coconut brushes, gourds and yabas. They asked what had happened to the money they had given Bedward.

Until this day no one knows what happened to the

money, for, when the police and soldiers laid hands on him, Bedward had no money in his pockets. He said he had sent it in advance up to Heaven.

It was the woman with the four eggs who had the last word.

'I've lost my h'eggs,' she said, 'but the world hasn't h'ended and I'm glad for it.'

Why the Wasp Can't Make Honey

You may have often wondered why it is that the Wasp can make a hive but can't make honey, while the Bee can make both the hive and the honey. Well, let me tell you why.

In the days when the world was very young, all the animals and birds and insects, and even the fish, had to go to school to learn a trade. The humming bird learned how to weave nests, the Peenie Wallie learned how to glow in the dark, the lizard how to change his colour, and the hen how to lay eggs, and the cow how to give milk. Some animals, of course, were more industrious than others and learnt all kind of skills. And some, like the donkey, were just too lazy to be bothered and learned hardly anything at all, which is why the donkey has remained a beast of burden to this very day.

Two pupils who showed special ability were the Wasp and the Bee. Wasp was very quick to learn but he was rather vain and mischievous. He was always playing pranks in class and upsetting the other students. Bee, on the other hand, thought things out more slowly, but was patient and industrious.

Both Wasp and Bee were soon in the very top class in the school. The teacher was an elderly Mongoose with a slight stoop, and glasses that were always falling down the end of his nose. He believed in strict discipline for he was teaching very advanced subjects—Nest-weaving, Hive-building, and Honey-making. He kept very good order among the several humming birds, doctor birds, and ants in the class.

Wasp rather enjoyed the Hive-building and could make a hive much faster than anyone else. He became quite boastful about this as though he had learnt all there was to know. While the other pupils were still poring over their books he would sneak off to the bottom of the playing field to smoke a cigar. Mongoose warned him that he would put him out of the class if this bad behaviour continued, but Wasp didn't pay any attention.

'How can they put me out of the class,' he boasted, 'when I am their best pupil? No one has such natural intelligence as I have. Why, I hardly need to study at all!'

At last the time came when the class was ready to move on to the next lesson—Honey-making. This was a very important part of the course and the teacher warned that the subject would come up in the examinations. He asked everyone to pay particular attention.

First of all, he told them, they must gather all the materials they would need. He set each pupil the task of gathering nectar from a different plant or flower.

Now Wasp, as I have said before, was a very vain fellow, always very elegantly dressed in a black and gold striped waistcoat and yellow kid gloves. He was

most careful not to spill anything on this waistcoat or soil his gloves. He was therefore very annoyed when he heard that he was expected to go digging into flowers to gather their nectar, which he knew was a nasty, messy, sticky kind of thing. 'And besides,' he thought with dismay, 'the pollen will ruin my waistcoat.'

Bee on the other hand set about his task very diligently. He put on a large leather apron, rolled his sleeves up to the elbow, tied a piece of cloth round his brow to stop the sweat running into his eyes and, thus prepared, humbly went off to labour in the fields.

'You look a real country bumpkin,' Wasp remarked scornfully when he saw Bee, 'you won't catch me going off to labour in the hot sun. I am going to have a day at the races.'

Wasp smoothed his waistcoat, smirked at himself in a little hand-mirror he always carried, and went off to enjoy himself. He backed three horses, won a large sum of money, and ended the day holding a party for his friends.

At school the next day, Mongoose took the nectar each pupil had gathered and measured it in a small silver balance. Bee had gathered more than anyone and the teacher was very pleased.

'You will be a good Honey-maker,' he praised him, 'because you are not afraid of hard work.'

Wasp was sitting at the back of the class trying not to catch the teacher's eye. He was beginning to feel very uncomfortable.

At last it was his turn to weigh his nectar.

'Now, Wasp,' Mongoose said sharply, 'turn out your pockets and let us see what you have brought.'

Wasp turned out his pockets. Out came a piece of string, two cigars, a fancy bottle-opener, a hand-mirror, and a ticket for the races—but no nectar.

The teacher was very angry indeed and in spite of all Wasp's pleas he promptly turned him out of the class. And that is why Wasp has never learned to make honey. He can make the hive but not the honey.

What is more, Wasp was so furious that he searched until he found a nice strong sting to put in his tail and then went buzzing around stinging people. Naturally this did not make him very popular.

Bee, however, finished school, passed all his exams in Honey-making, and set himself up in business. His children and grandchildren have carried on the family business ever since and have become very prosperous.

As for that idle fellow the Wasp, his children and grandchildren have only inherited his knowledge of how to build a hive—and his sting.

Woman is a People

A wedding in Jamaica is a very important occasion.

There is great eating and drinking, and singing and dancing, and of course much chat and gossip. A real country wedding must have a feast of curry goat, and there must be enough rum to keep everyone happy till morning. Everyone must be invited—relations, friends, neighbours, and even passing strangers—so it is no wonder that a wedding can cost much more than a poor man can afford.

This is why many Jamaicans, when they first get married, do not have the wedding celebration, but wait until they have saved up enough money for it. Sometimes this takes them all their lives, and when they are finally able to celebrate with the pomp and ceremony that the occasion demands, their children and even their grandchildren may be among the guests.

My Uncle Mizpah had a wedding like that. He and my Aunt Mattie had been married for nearly fifty years, but with fourteen children in the family there never seemed to be enough money to spare for a wedding feast. Aunt Mattie never stopped grumbling about it.

Aunt Mattie was a great grumbler. With fourteen children to grumble at she got plenty of practice. Uncle Mizpah could never do anything right. If he stayed at home she accused him of getting under her feet all day. If he went to the rum shop she was angry because he was out enjoying himself while she had to stay at home. If the sun was shining it was too hot and if the sun was not shining it was too cold. There was no pleasing Aunt Mattie at all.

When they did finally set a date for the wedding feast, Aunt Mattie grumbled more and more. When Uncle Mizpah suggested that they should have it in April, she asked him how he expected her to be ready so soon. When he suggested October instead, she wanted to know why he was delaying it so long. They finally agreed that it should be in June, but that didn't put an end to Aunt Mattie's grumbling. Oh no! Far from it!

When Mizpah showed Aunt Mattie the suit he had had made for the occasion, she took one look at it, rubbed the cloth between finger and thumb, sniffed it, and remarked scornfully,

'Did you say a tailor made that, or an architect for human clothes?'

And when Mizpah brought home the goat that was to provide the curry goat feast, Aunt Mattie cast an eye over the animal and declared,

'Lawd, how it maugre! Its bones knock together like dominoes.'

And if Mizpah dared poke his head round the kitchen door, where for the past month Aunt Mattie had been soaking the dried fruit in rum for the cake, and dared to ask if she were busy, she cracked back at him,

'Me busy? Me make a dog with fleas look like it's taking a holiday.'

After that Uncle Mizpah gave up and went off to the rum shop in the village for a quiet game of dominoes.

As he walked along the road he began to complain to himself about how women were always grumbling.

'Woman are a people who can't do anything without dem grumble,' he muttered to himself. 'If dem walk, dem a-grumble. If dem talk, dem a-grumble. If dem eat, dem a-grumble. If dem sing, dem a-grumble. Grumble too much, man, grumble too much.'

Now the village samfi man heard Uncle Mizpah, and being an idle fellow with nothing better to do, began to make up a song about his troubles. The song went like this:

Woman is a people
Woman is a people

Dem a-walk, dem a-grumble
Dem a-eat, dem a-grumble
Dem a-sing, dem a-grumble
Dem a-sleep, dem a-grumble

Grumble too much
Grumble too much.

The song had a very catchy tune, and by the time Uncle Mizpah got to the rum shop the song had reached there before him. In Jamaica a new song spreads faster than love-bush. And as it spread everyone in the village made up a verse or two of their own. I won't bother telling you all the verses they made up.

The day of the wedding feast, which was set for a Saturday, drew near. By Wednesday the relations began arriving from all over the countryside, getting Aunt Mattie even more hot and bothered. The village dressmaker was making her a wedding dress of purple satin and a hat with huge peacock feathers, but at the last moment Aunt Mattie thought she would look better in plum coloured velvet. And perhaps a hat with three pink roses. The dressmaker, who had nearly swallowed five pins in her struggle to get a tape measure round Aunt Mattie and didn't want to risk swallowing any more, persuaded her to keep the purple satin dress. Aunt Mattie, however, insisted on adding three pink roses to the hat with peacock feathers.

By this time the whole village was watching everything Aunt Mattie did with great glee and every time she grumbled about something a new verse was added to the song:

Dem a-dress, dem a-grumble
Purple satin, dem a-grumble
Peacock feathers, dem a-grumble
Grumble too much
Grumble too much.

When the great day finally came, Uncle Mizpah and Aunt Mattie went to church surrounded by their fourteen children and twenty-seven grandchildren.

The pastor blessed the couple and hoped that the union would prove fruitful. Then the fun began.

What a feast there was! Curry goat, plantains, yams, breadfruit, sweet potatoes, pumpkins, green bananas, and for the children lemonade and bun and cheese. The village band, after much coughing and scraping of their throats, which they referred to as 'tuning', began to play quadrilles. The guests jumped up and down so violently on the dance floor that the house shook.

By this time the men had drunk a great deal of rum and were getting bold. One of them began to hum:

Woman is a people
Woman is a people

His wife dug him sharply in the ribs to shut him up, but another man continued singing softly:

Dem a-pray, dem a-grumble
Dem a-gossip, dem a-grumble

Someone on the other side of the table took it up:

Dem a-marry, dem a-grumble
Dem a-dress, dem a-grumble

Quick as love-bush the song spread among the wedding guests:

Purple-satin, dem a-grumble
Peacock feathers, dem a-grumble

Until the whole company was singing:

Curry goat, dem a-grumble
Three pink roses, dem a-grumble

Uncle Mizpah felt he wanted to sink under the table and hide from sight. He made a face at the singers and tried to frown them down but it is easier to stop a herd of pigs in a field of pumpkins than a good song when it has got going.

In vain he shouted 'Kendal' and 'Bog Walk'. These are the names of stations at the end of railway lines in Jamaica and to shout 'Kendal' or 'Bog Walk' is a way of shouting 'Stop! Enough!' But it was of no use.

By now the musicians had picked up the tune and were scraping their fiddles, blowing their flutes and banging their drums in time with the wedding guests, who were simply roaring at the top of their voices:

Married woman, dem a-grumble
Single woman, dem a-grumble
Fat woman, dem a-grumble

Uncle Mizpah did not dare look at Aunt Mattie.

Pretty woman, dem a-grumble
Ugly woman, dem a-grumble
All breed of woman, dem a-grumble

Everyone was singing, swaying and stamping feet. The

village blacksmith was singing soprano. Big, fat Miss Netty who kept the village grocery shop was singing bass, and the chorus came roaring out at the end of each verse:

> Grumble too much
> Grumble too much.

Uncle Mizpah at last dared to look at Aunt Mattie. Her face looked like John Crow. Whatever would she say to him afterwards. Uncle Mizpah trembled at the thought. But in our darkest moments the Good Lord sends us inspiration. As the last chorus came to an end, Uncle Mizpah suddenly jumped up and sang a verse of his own:

> From Adam time, dem grumble
> Till Judgement Day, dem grumble
> But we love dem when dem grumble
> Yes, we love dem when dem grumble.

The wedding guests burst out laughing and clapped their hands and stamped their feet, delighted at how Uncle Mizpah had saved the day.

Uncle Mizpah looked at Aunt Mattie. Her face no longer looked like John Crow. She was laughing heartily. She laughed so much that she split her purple satin dress, and the hat with the peacock feathers and three pink roses fell over one eye. Aunt Mattie knew that the joke was on herself and that a wise woman must

share it. Uncle Mizpah clasped her round the waist and planted a kiss on her cheek.

The only thing to do in such a situation was to sing the song all over again from the beginning which everyone did, Aunt Mattie joining in as heartily as the rest.

From that day onwards, whenever Aunt Mattie grumbled too much, Uncle Mizpah had only to look at her and hum a verse of the song for her to laugh and recover her good humour.

The only thing she never forgave him for was for making her split the purple satin dress with laughing so much, but she has worn the hat with the peacock feathers and three pink roses at the christening of her twenty-eighth, twenty-ninth, and thirtieth grandchild.

Water in the Gourd

Mas' Eddy was a small farmer. Each morning he rose very early to work on his land which lay five chains from his home. Before he left, his wife, Dulcimena, cooked him some yam and roasted breadfruit to take with him for his breakfast.

'Only fool man work on empty stomick,' she would say, 'make sure you stop to eat.'

Dulcimena also gave him a big gourd filled with water. Mas' Eddie was very proud of this gourd. It was a very big gourd that he had picked off a calabash tree near the sea one year.

One morning—it was a Tuesday—Mas' Eddy got up as usual to go to work in his field. First he tied his trousers above the ankle with string, then he filled his pockets with the yam and roasted breadfruit, slung the gourd of water over his shoulder and picked up his hoe and cutlass. He wrapped the handle of the cutlass in paper and put it on the top of his head. He always carried his cutlass that way.

On the way to his field he stopped a few times to chat with people on the road and so the sun had already risen when he got there. Mas' Eddy hung his gourd on the branch of a tree by its string and set to work right away. He worked very busily for a couple of hours, clearing the land with his cutlass, digging holes with his hoe, and planting some corn he had brought with him. The ants were particularly troublesome this year and he stopped from time to time to brush them off his trouser legs. By eleven o'clock in the morning he was hot and thirsty. He decided to stop for a drink of water and some breadfruit.

He went to the tree to get the gourd but to his astonishment it wasn't there.

'But how can it have gone?' muttered Mas' Eddy to himself, wrinkling his forehead. 'No one has been here but me. A duppy must have taken it.'

Duppies, as everyone knows, are fond of playing those kind of tricks on people.

He was just about to turn away in disappointment when he noticed something. The string, which had been tied round the neck of the gourd, was still hanging down from the tree. And it was hanging down very stiffly as though something heavy were on the end of it. Mas' Eddy went a little closer and took a good look. His eyes turned crossways and his grey hairs curled even tighter to his head. The ants had eaten away the gourd—all except a tiny piece of the neck held by the string—but the water was still hanging in mid-air.

Mas' Eddy walked round and round the tree but each time that he came back to the same place the water was still there. It was rounded in shape like the gourd and the sun glistened on its sides. The only problem was how Mas' Eddy was to drink it.

'If I try to pick it up in my hands,' he thought, 'my

hands will simply go through the water. And if I untie the string the water may fall to the ground. I had better suck it up.'

So Mas' Eddy stood right underneath the water, pressed his lips to its side and sucked. The water slid down his hot, parched throat—cool, liquid, and sweet. He sucked and sucked until finally the string bobbed lightly up and down with no weight on the end of it at all. Mas' Eddy had drunk all the water.

And that of course was his big mistake. Obviously he should have left the water hanging there and called his neighbours to come and look at it. Because to this day no one believes that the ants ate up his gourd and left the water hanging by a string.

The only person who believes Mas' Eddy is his wife Dulcimena. Ask Dulcimena if it happened and she will reply with a shrug of her shoulders: 'Anything could happen to that fool man,' and go back to boiling her yams.

Lovers' Leap

On the south coast of Jamaica, in the parish of St Elizabeth, is a great cliff which rises hundreds of feet above the sea. From here one can see the whole south coast of the island spread far below. The highest point on this cliff is known as Lovers' Leap.

Over 200 years ago Lovers' Leap was called Pedro Point, the highest point on the great Pedro Bluff. A look-out was kept there to give warning of pirate or enemy ships, for Jamaica was attacked from time to time by the Spanish and French fleets which came sweeping round the western end of the island. The story of how its name got changed to Lovers' Leap is a tragic one.

At the time of our story, Pedro Point was on the property of a very wealthy planter, Mister Josiah Yardley. The name of this property was Yardley Chase.

Mister Josiah Yardley was a very hard man—hard in his business dealings with his fellow planters and harsh in his treatment of his slaves. Above all Mister Josiah Yardley liked to be obeyed. If he had ever been asked to sum up his religion in one word, that word would have been obedience.

In those troubled times, Mister Yardley kept one of his slaves as a permanent look-out on Pedro Point to watch for enemy ships. The slave he had chosen for this important job was Kunu John. Kunu John had been a prince among his own people in Africa and had not taken kindly to a life of slavery. In spite of the most terrible punishments he refused to work in the fields with the other slaves. Mister Yardley finally decided to make him the look-out on Pedro Point for Kunu John was brave and strong and could be trusted to keep a sharp watch.

So Kunu spent his days and nights on the great cliff. The cliff was so high that at night the moon seemed to hang only half way up the sky and in the daytime he could even look down on the rainbow shimmering below in the misty spray of the sea. Here on the great cliff Kunu could imagine that he was free again and not a slave.

But Kunu was not always alone. One of the house slaves, a very pretty quadroon girl called Tansy, used to steal out at night to see him. Kunu and Tansy loved each other. When all thirty-two of her pearly white teeth flashed a smile at him, Kunu's heart shimmied like the end of the rainbow. Kunu and Tansy swore that they would never be parted.

But Mister Josiah Yardley had other ideas about that. The day came when the country was at peace at last, and it was no longer necessary to keep a look-out on the cliff. He wondered what to do with Kunu John. Kunu, he was sure, would always give trouble if brought back to work in the fields, but he was a big, strong fellow and would fetch a handsome price in the

Slave Market. Mister Yardley decided to sell Kunu John.

It was Tansy who heard the news first from the other slaves. Mister Yardley was going to sell Kunu in the Slave Market in Spanishtown when he next visited the capital. Tansy felt that her heart would burst. She stole out of the house and slipped through the mango trees at the bottom of the garden until she was on the red dirt track that led up to Pedro Point. Then her heels flew. By the time she reached the cliff she was out of breath and had a sharp pain in her side.

'Kunu! Kunu!' she cried.

Kunu John rose from where he had been sitting on a small ledge just below the edge of the cliff. Gently he helped her down. Here they would be hidden from sight and could talk in peace. He placed some wild flowers he had been gathering in her lap. Still sobbing, Tansy told him the terrible news and as she spoke Kunu's face grew dark and stern.

'They shall never sell me again in the Slave Market,' he said fiercely, 'I shall die first.'

Tansy threw her arms round his neck.

'If you go away, Kunu,' she whispered, 'I shall kill myself. I cannot live without you.'

Kunu sat for a long time without saying anything. At last he spoke:

'Listen, Tansy,' he said, 'my people in Africa have a story about the Moon. In the days when the world was very young the Sun and the Moon were always quarrelling with each other. The Moon felt that the

Sun had a much better time of it than she because there was more going on in the daytime. People were eating and working and fighting and playing and laughing and talking, and the Sun could look on and enjoy it all. When the Moon finally rose in the sky there was only the whistling of the crickets and the singing of the tree frogs to keep her company. The rest of the world was asleep. At last she could stand it no longer and went to complain to the Great Earth Mother.'

' "Great Earth Mother," the Moon said, "you have divided things very unfairly. The sun has all the fun watching babies playing with their toes in the mud. He listens to the women gossiping as they grind corn, and men singing as they hollow out a canoe for the river. He shines on the weavers weaving their cloth and the warriors sharpening their spears. Whereas by the time I am half-way up the sky, everyone is yawning their heads off and stretching tired limbs, and before I have even settled my lamp for the night everyone is fast asleep. What fun is that for anyone! All I see is an occasional pair of lovers—and they are too interested in each other to be much company for anyone!" '

'The Great Earth Mother smiled when she heard the Moon's complaint. "Daughter," she said, "do not be discontented with your lot. It is true that the sun has all the hustle and bustle of the work-a-day world but you have a special charge over all brave men who seek freedom. You must shine to give them hope and courage. As you go up the sky, it will be a sign to them that there is another world beyond the grave. And it

will be a sign to lovers that they can find eternal love together if they choose." '

While Kunu had been telling his story the conch had blown to signal the end of work in the fields. It was already evening.

'You must go back to the house soon, Tansy,' Kunu said gently, 'they may miss you and then you would be in trouble.'

'And you, Kunu, what will you do?'

Kunu smiled. 'When the Moon rises, Tansy, I shall jump off the cliff. Better death than a life of slavery and separation from you. That way I shall be free.'

Tansy clung even closer to him. 'Let me jump with you, Kunu. Let us jump together, then no man can part us ever again.'

The next morning Mister Yardley got up as usual and called for Tansy to bring him his hot water. But there was no Tansy. Mister Yardley was annoyed. In a very bad temper he went up to Pedro Point to find Kunu John and tell him that he was going to sell him in the Slave Market in Spanishtown but there was no Kunu John either. Mister Yardley was furious. He rode all over his property asking if anyone had seen the missing couple. Only a half crazy old woman who lived by herself in a little hut near the cliff edge could tell him anything at all. Last night she had gone out to gather herbs and had seen two figures jump together over the edge of the cliff. The Moon had caught them up in a great golden net, she said, and when she looked again she had seen them walking on the Moon.

Mister Yardley did not believe such stories, of course. He was far too hard headed a man for such foolishness, but he could not stop his slaves from believing them. Nor could he stop them from changing the name of Pedro Point to Lovers' Leap. However much he threatened and forbade it, the whole countryside went on calling it Lovers' Leap, and long after Mister Yardley died and was buried in the churchyard at Southfields people still went on calling it Lovers' Leap and have done so to this very day.

The Big Potato

My friend Herbie liked to try out new things. He had a piece of land beside the railway line near to the level crossing. I was the gate-keeper at this level crossing, and sometimes of an evening we used to lean on the gate chatting and smoking our pipes.

One evening Herbie came home quite late because he had been to an agricultural class for small farmers that was held once a week in Maypen. He was carrying something in a paper bag.

'What have you got there, Herbie?' I called out when I saw him.

'Wait till you see,' Herbie replied excitedly, 'It's a new variety of potato. The Agricultural Inspector gave one to me to try out on my land. They grow bigger than any potato you've ever seen.'

'Cho, man, those government inspectors tell you one whole heap of foolishness. It won't grow any bigger than any other potato.'

'Yes, it will. It's a new variety from Japan. I'm going to plant it right beside the railway line so that you can watch it grow.'

I didn't argue any more and to tell the truth I forgot about the matter. Herbie was always trying out something new. The whole countryside round about used to laugh at Herbie's new methods of farming.

About a week later I got up one morning at six o'clock as usual to open the gates of the level crossing. The Maypen to Kingston train passed through at ten past six each morning. I could already hear the train whistle in the distance. But this morning things were not as usual. Something had happened in the night to make the whole crossing rise up in the air. In fact one could not call it a *level* crossing any longer. It looked more like a small mountain.

What is more, there was a whole crowd of people gathered in the road on either side of the track. A boy had fallen off his bike in astonishment, and the shock had made an old woman let go of the goat she was leading to market. She was now chasing after it trying to catch the animal. On the far side of the line the driver of a mulecart was having trouble, too. The animal had its ears laid back and was backing away from the crossing getting more and more entangled in the traces. The driver was shouting at it to get on.

At that moment the train came puffing up and stopped with a screech of brakes when the driver realized that the gates were not open for him. He clanged his bell when he saw what had happened to the crossing.

'Who put that mountain in the middle of the track?' he shouted angrily.

Even in the few minutes I had been standing there the mound had certainly grown bigger and now the railway lines were cracking and bending with the strain as they were forced slowly but steadily up in the air.

'Lawd me God!' squawked Miss Betsy who taught Sunday School, 'It's a warning to us. The end of the world is near.'

It was now after six o'clock in the morning, and more and more people whose way to work took them over the level crossing were stopping to gape at the mound in the road. There was a long line of cars and trucks held up on either side of the line. Children with school bags, bread-cart men, fish vendors, women with buckets of water, men with loads of bananas on their heads were all milling round in the road laughing and talking.

In the midst of all this confusion I suddenly felt a tug on my elbow. It was Herbie. I could see by his face that he was a very worried man. 'Ebenezer,' he whispered, 'it's the potato.'

'What about the potato?' I asked quite bewildered.

'The big potato. The one I planted by the railway line. It's grown right under the line and pushed it up in the air.'

I looked very hard at the mound in the middle of the crossing. It had cracked open on top and sure enough one or two green shoots were sprouting through.

'It's a judgement on us,' Miss Betsy was saying over and over again, 'a judgement on us.'

'The Government's to blame,' a truck driver shouted angrily. 'If it's not potholes in the road, it's mountains. What will happen next?'

'There must have been an earthquake in the middle of the night.'

Everyone was shouting at once.

Just then the District Constable rode up on his bicycle clanging the bell.

'Why are you people blocking the road?' he asked angrily. 'Move along there, move along.'

A young girl giggled pertly.

'How can we move along with that thing in the middle of the road?' she asked. 'Lawd, I wish me Mammy were here to see it.'

The District Constable set eyes on me.

'Mr Ebenezer,' he called, 'what has occured at your level crossing? Why has it gone up in the air like that?'

Herbie came to my rescue.

'You see, Constable,' he said nervously, 'I planted a potato last week . . .'

'I don't care if you planted pigs, cows and your grandmother last week, Mr Herbison. That has nothing to do with the case. I'm asking Mr Ebenezer what has happened at his level crossing.'

'But that's just it, Constable. The potato grew bigger and bigger under the track and swelled and swelled and forced the line up in the air.'

The Constable looked very serious.

'If what you say is true, you are in trouble, Mr Herbison. You can be charged with wilful destruction of public property. But whoever heard of a potato growing that big?'

'Take a look for yourself, Constable,' I implored,

'If that isn't a potato under the railway line, what is it?'

The Constable went up to the mound in the middle of the crossing. The crowd helped him scramble up its side with a few pushes and shoves. Finally he stood right on top of the mountain and looked down through the crack. Underneath was something big and brown and knobbly—just like a potato. The Constable drew breath:

'Anyone with intelligence can see immediately what the trouble is,' he announced importantly. 'It's a big potato—that's all. We'll have to send for a digger to dig it out.'

That day was surely the longest day of my life.

First they sent for a digger. The machine dug and scraped and scraped and dug but couldn't lift the potato.

Then they sent for a crane. The crane tugged and lifted and lifted and tugged but couldn't pull out the potato.

Then they sent for a wrecker. The wrecker tied chains round the potato and pulled and strained and strained and pulled but it couldn't budge the potato.

Then they sent for two fire engines from Maypen. The firemen put ladders against its sides and hosed the potato down with water but they couldn't wash it away.

Then they sent for a regiment of soldiers and the soldiers hacked and chipped and chipped and hacked, but as fast as they hacked and chipped the potato just grew and grew.

Then they sent for the Governor General who made a speech about a national emergency and took the salute with his sword and plumed hat, but that didn't move the potato.

Finally in desperation they sent for some dynamite.

Bang! Boom! Boom! Bang!

They blasted and they blasted and the potato went up in the air raining bits and pieces of potato over the whole countryside. You should have seen the mess my level crossing was in by the time they had finished.

Herbie was naturally very frightened that he might be put in prison for disrupting the railway line with a giant potato. The District Constable was just itching to arrest someone. He hadn't had the chance to arrest anyone for two years and three months. The Governor General, however, was more cautious. He called Herbie to him.

'Tell me,' he inquired, 'where did you get a potato like that in the first place?'

'I got it from the Government, Your Excellency,' stammered Herbie, 'The Government Agricultural Inspector gave it to me.'

The Governor General looked very thoughtful. He looked very thoughtful for quite some minutes.

Herbie waited trembling, sure that he was about to be arrested.

Finally the Governor General said:

'I think, Mr Herbison, that you should go home and not plant any more potatoes.'

Amazed at getting off so lightly, Herbie turned

quickly to get as far from the scene as possible. The Governor General took his arm.

'And just one more thing, Mr Herbison,' he murmured in his ear, 'there is no need to go spreading rumours that it was a Government potato. I suggest that you forget about the whole affair.'

Forget about the whole affair? Was Herbie glad to do that!

From that day on Herbie planted no more potatoes but he didn't lose his interest in trying out new things. Last year his cow gave birth to four ducks, five hens, and a guinea pig.

Pickwa and the Duppy

In the days before there were a lot of motor cars in Jamaica, duppies were seen rather more often than they are today.

People used to see them sitting in churchyards nursing their babies, running behind the cane cart to pick up bits of juicy sugar cane, and going off to market on Saturdays to buy their yams and sweet potatoes.

Duppies can be very provoking, of course. A man riding a mule along a country road at night may suddenly feel two arms go round his waist. A duppy is having a free ride on the back of his mule. Sometimes when boys are swimming in the river duppies go and sit on their heads and push them under the water. They also like to pull people's noses to make them longer. Yes, duppies can be a nuisance. Take the case of Pickwa.

Pickwa was a boy who loved roseapples, and roseapples grow by the sides of rivers. One day Pickwa had gone to his favourite roseapple tree and, seeing a very big fruit high up in the tree, he climbed and climbed until he was within reach of the lovely, big, yellow-green roseapple. Pickwa could already feel his teeth biting into it.

But just as he was about to take a bite he heard a chuckle and there sitting at the foot of the tree, with his hands folded across his tummy, was the fattest duppy Pickwa had ever seen. Pickwa's knees began to tremble violently and his head grew bigger with fright as he clung to his high branch.

'Throw down the apple to me, Pickwa,' the duppy called, 'I have been waiting all day for someone to climb the tree and get it for me.'

Pickwa looked at the apple and then he looked at the duppy. It was unwise not to do what the duppy said, for duppies made bad enemies. At the same time he felt that he could not bear to give up the roseapple. But Pickwa was a clever boy and he had an idea.

'Certainly, Mas' Duppy,' he called back, 'you can have this roseapple but I see another one that is even fatter and juicier on the next branch. Let me throw that down first.'

Pickwa climbed, picked the fruit, and threw it down to the duppy. The duppy ate it so fast he could hardly have tasted it.

'That was a very good roseapple, Pickwa,' the duppy called, 'Now give me the one in your hand.'

'Certainly, Mas' Duppy,' Pickwa replied politely, 'but it will taste even better if you try a few others first. Let me shake some down to you.'

As he spoke he gave a branch a mighty shake and the apples came tumbling down. The duppy ran round the tree gathering them up and stuffing them into his mouth as fast as he could go.

'Those were not quite ripe,' he called to Pickwa, 'try the next branch.'

'Certainly, Mas' Duppy,' Pickwa replied, 'these on the next branch are very juicy.' Once again he sent down a shower of roseapples. The greedy duppy swallowed them all whole, not even noticing that some were not ripe at all.

For nearly half an hour Pickwa worked furiously picking roseapples for the duppy. He counted that the duppy had now eaten sixty-three roseapples, and some of them had been very green ones.

As everyone knows, duppies are generally a pale white colour. In the daytime it is sometimes difficult to see them because the sun shines right through them. This duppy, however, was white no longer. He had turned a delicate green. He still kept eating the rose-apples Pickwa sent down to him but much more slowly.

Pickwa climbed higher and higher in the tree shaking down more and more fruit. The duppy was sitting in the middle of a great heap of roseapples but he seemed to be losing his appetite. Finally he gave up altogether and groaned.

'I have a pain in my side, Pickwa,' he called piteously, 'get me some water.'

Pickwa came down the tree and ran to the river. He filled his schoolbag with water and brought it back to the duppy. The duppy was now lying with his legs kicking in the air and his eyes tight shut. He was groaning and holding his stomach.

'I must have eaten too many roseapples,' he gasped as Pickwa splashed water on him, 'run for the doctor, boy.'

'Certainly, Mas' Duppy,' said Pickwa, 'but wouldn't you like to eat this last, big, juicy roseapple before I go?' He held out the one he had had in his hand all this time.

But the duppy shut his eyes and shook his head. 'No,' he shuddered, 'throw it in the river, boy. I never want to see another roseapple again.'

At that Pickwa picked up his school bag, crammed the roseapple into it, and ran for his life, never once looking back to see if the duppy was following him. But the duppy wasn't following him. The duppy was rolling over and over in the grass until finally he rolled right into the river and sank like a bag of roseapples.

When Pickwa reached home his mother took the roseapple and made it into a big roseapple pie, and he and his eleven brothers and sisters had it for supper.